Create the Life of Your Drea... Board for Unleashing Your Creativity

My dear believer:

Welcome to a journey of self discovery, creativity, and the power of visualization. This book isn't just about crafting a vision board; it's about crafting a life that reflects your deepest passions and dreams.

Whether you're an artist, writer, musician, or simply someone with a desire to express yourself creatively, you're about to embark on a path that will help you bring your inner world to life.

What is a Vision Board?

At its core, a vision board is a visual representation of your goals, dreams, and desires. It's a powerful tool that allows you to focus your energy on what you want to attract into your life.

By placing images, words, and symbols that resonate with your creative aspirations on a board, you create a tangible reminder of what you're working towards. But a vision board is more than just a collection of pretty pictures: it's a manifestation of your intentions, a daily source of inspiration, and a way to keep your creative goals front and center.

Let's embark on this journey together toward becoming our best selves!

Sending you a big hug,
Antonella.

Unleash Your Creative Potential:
Free Vision Board Toolkit

Welcome to a world where your dreams take center stage, and your creativity knows no bounds. As a special gift to you, we've created a comprehensive Vision Board Toolkit that complements everything you'll explore in this book.

This downloadable resource is packed with exclusive content designed to help you dive deeper into your creative journey and manifest the life you've always envisioned.

Why Download This Toolkit?

- **Exclusive Exercises:** Discover in-depth self-discovery exercises that will guide you in identifying your unique talents and passions.
- **Visual Tools and Templates:** Get access to beautifully designed templates and tools that make creating your vision board easy and inspiring.
- **Inspiration and Motivation:** Explore stories, prompts, and techniques that will keep your creative fire burning brightly.
- **Step-by-Step Guidance:** Learn how to use this book and the toolkit together to create a vision board that truly resonates with your creative soul.

This toolkit is your companion on the journey to living a creatively fulfilled life. Don't miss out! Download it now and start creating with purpose.

To use a QR code, simply open your smartphone's camera and point it at the code. Your device will automatically scan it and direct you to the linked content. You can also access by sending a mail to me at antonellabontempi.comercial@gmail.com

Future Past

Create.
Work.
Inspire.

YOU
GOT
THIS

INSPIRE,
EMPOWER,
ENJOY

"Everything you've ever wanted is on the other side of FEAR!"

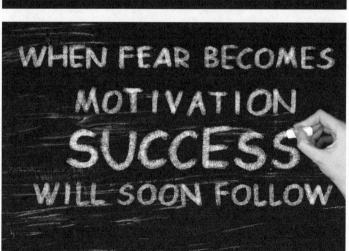

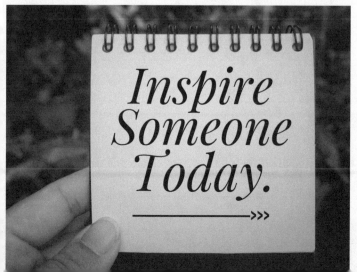

RESILIENCE

I LIKE MY BODY

I'M BEAUTIFUL

I'M FIT

self

acceptance

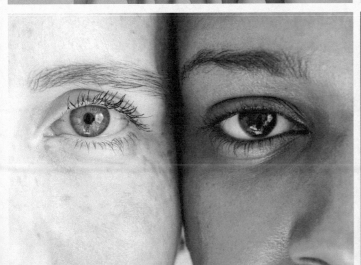

ACCEPT RISK

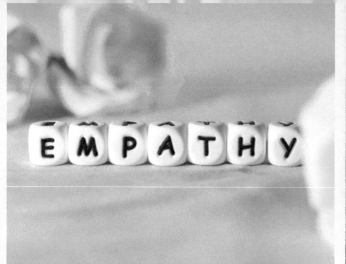

listen with empathy

care

LIFESTYLE CHANGE →

Failure is success in progress

YOUR MINDSET MATTERS

education social leadership growth
strategy attitude enable
business support mindset career
respect control process opportunity motivation women
psychology beliefs community
authority multi-dimensional
empowerment
confidence accountability
initiative self-esteem self-determination
gender power group information decision responsibility
autonomy

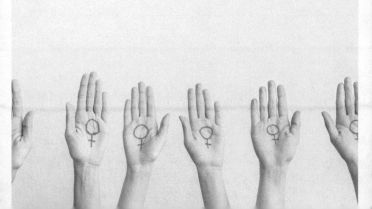

GRLPWR

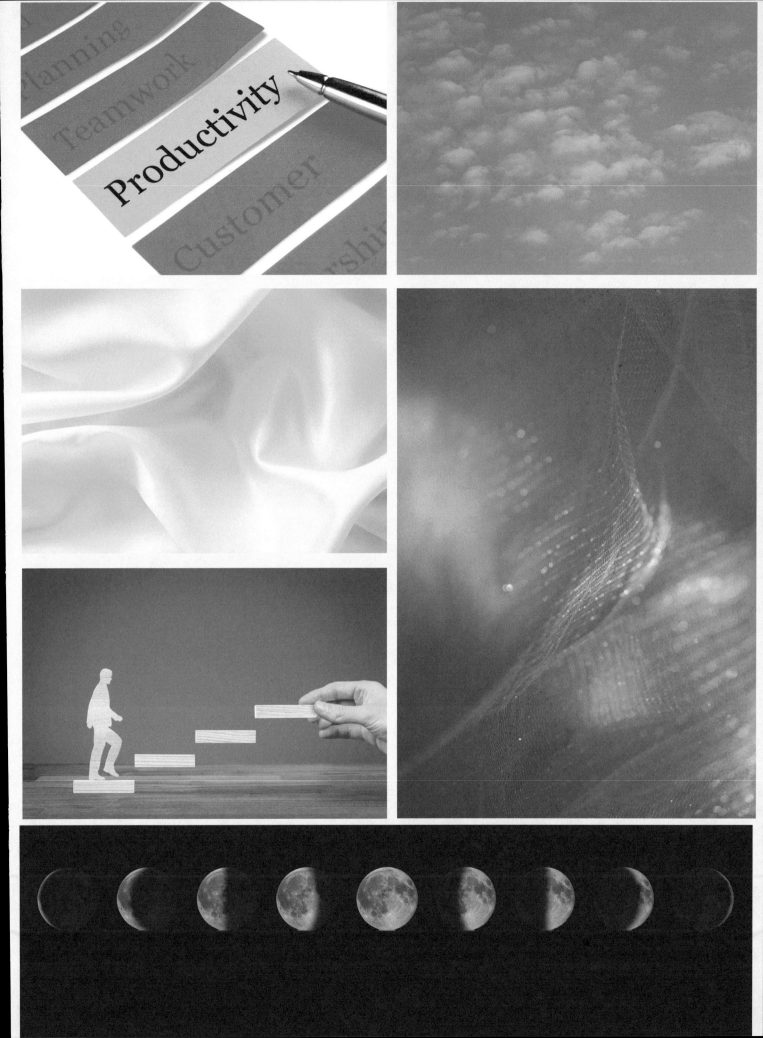

HOPE

inspire

NOW or NEVER

BELIEVE IN YOURSELF

You can't

BE CREATIVE

good things take time

INSPIRE OTHERS

YOU CAN DO iT!

you ☑ can do anything

Keep Going!

Believe in Yourself!

Stay Focused!

NEVER Give up

Self-care
IS EMPOWERMENT

SELF CARE

SELF LOVE

meditate

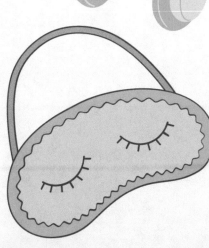

yoga

it's TIME -TO- Relax

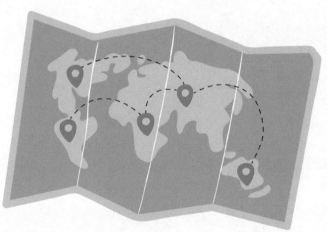

TIME TO TRAVEL

LOS ANGELES

TOKYO

NEW YORK

SÃO PAOLO

LONDON
PARIS
FRANKFURT
ROME

DELHI

MOSCOW

TORONTO

TICKET

TICKET

ne Army Raden Sudirma
24 January 1916[a] - 29
ng Indonesian military
n National Revolution
nesian National Arme
respected
Purbalingga, Dutch
dcap in 1916 and
gent student at a
ame respected within th
Islam. After dropping ou
6 he began working as a teacher an
dmaster at Muhammadiyah run elementary
the Japanese occupied the Indies in 1942,
to teach before joining
sored Defenders of the Home
nder in Banyumas in 1944
rebel for by his fello
ned in Bogor. Afte
dence on 17 August
t to Jakarta to m
overseeing the
Banyumas the
body
cide

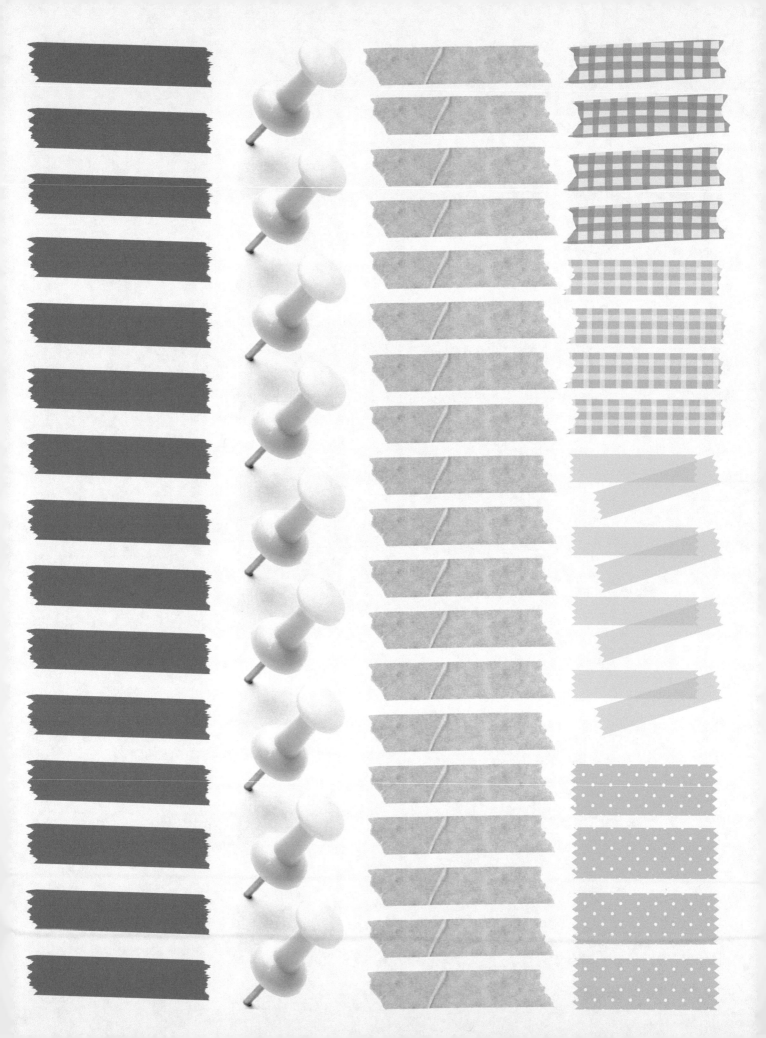

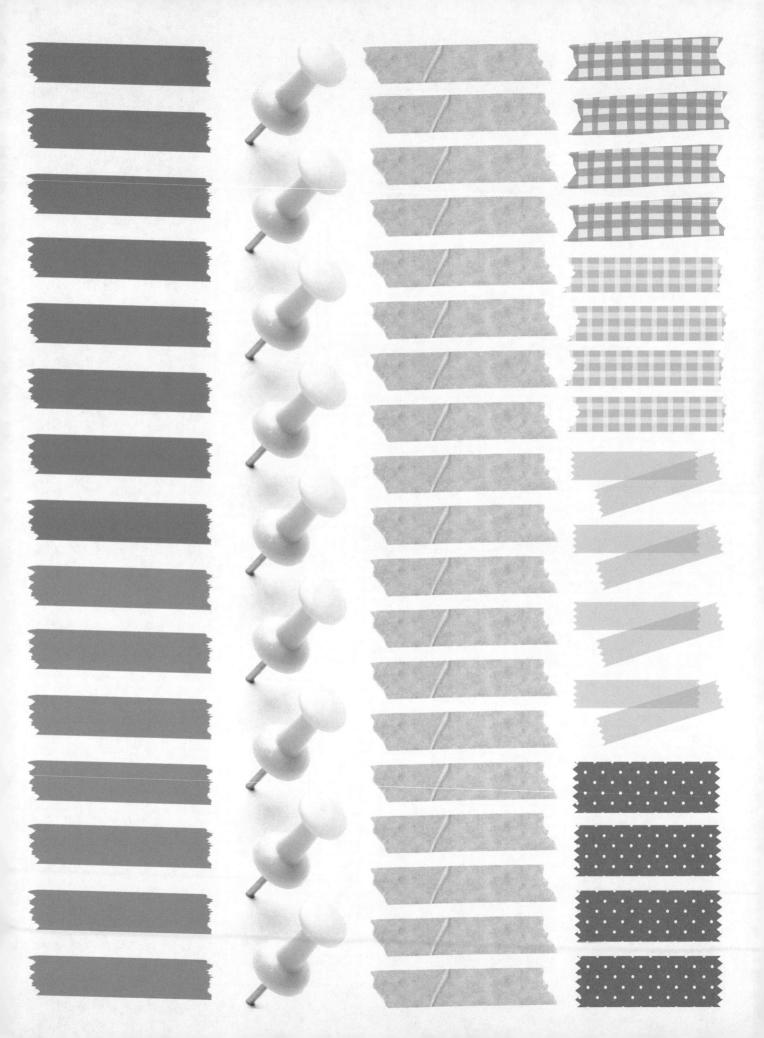